BLANK COMIC BOOK

BELONGS TO

____

____

STORY TITLE:

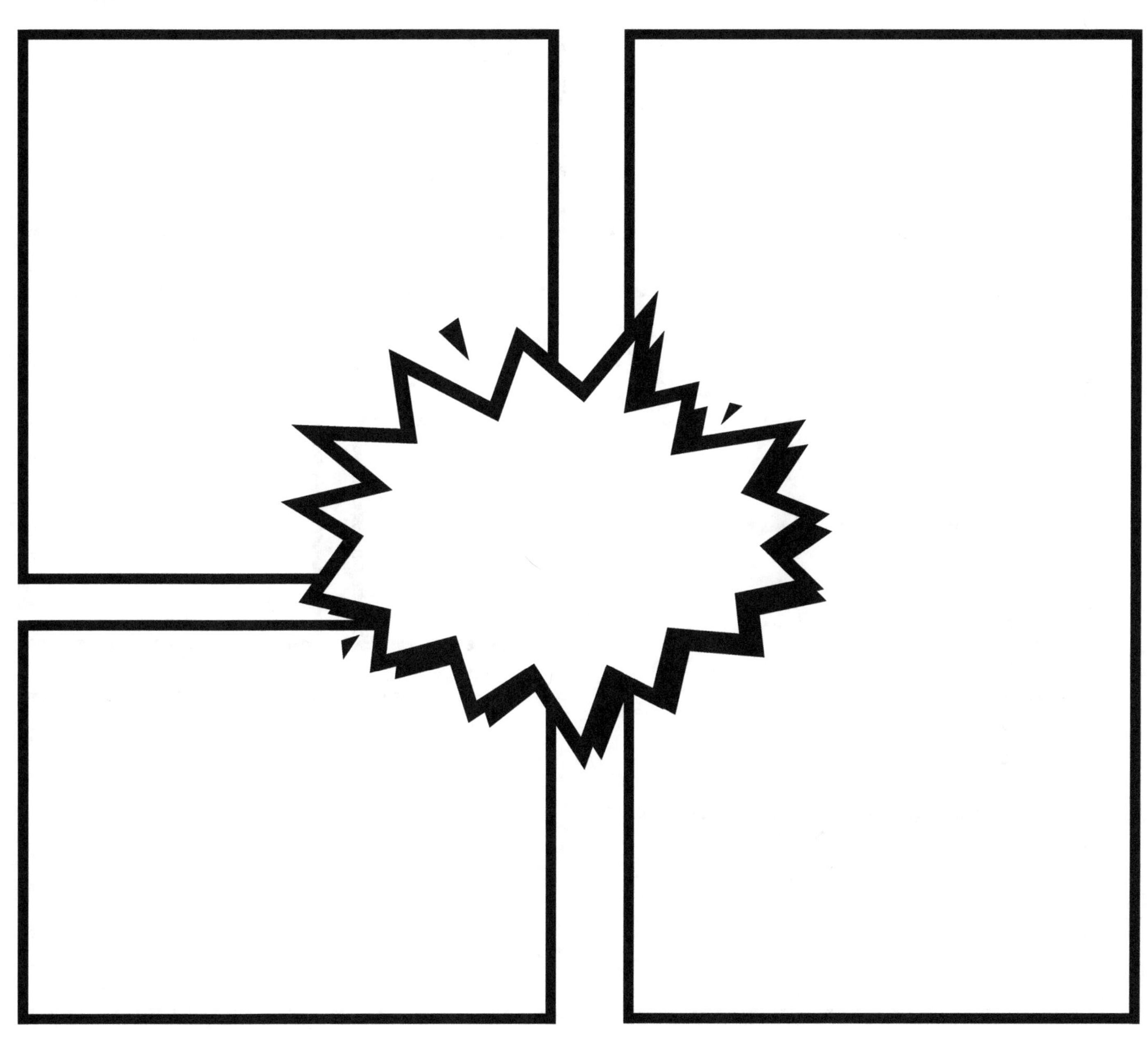

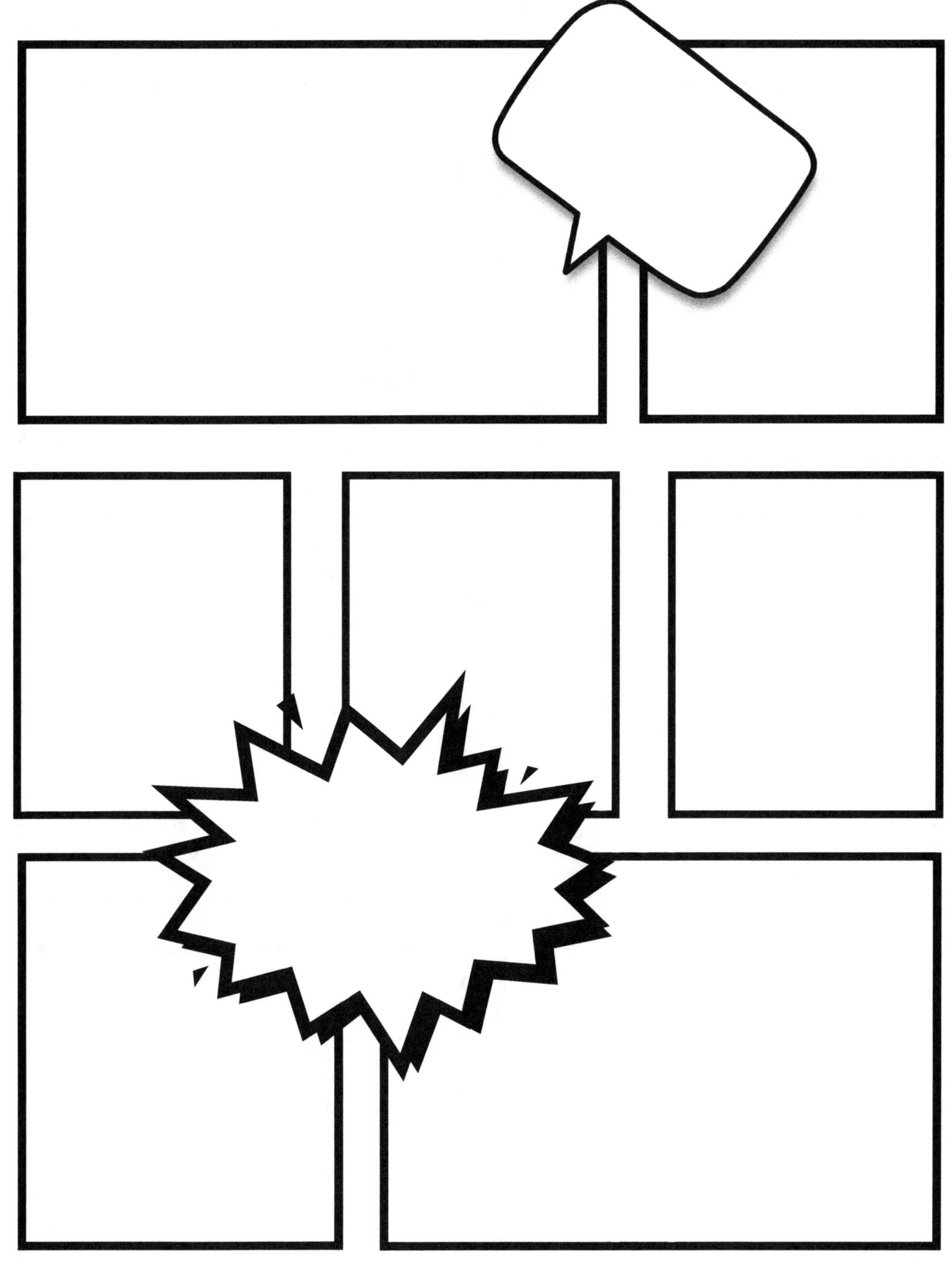

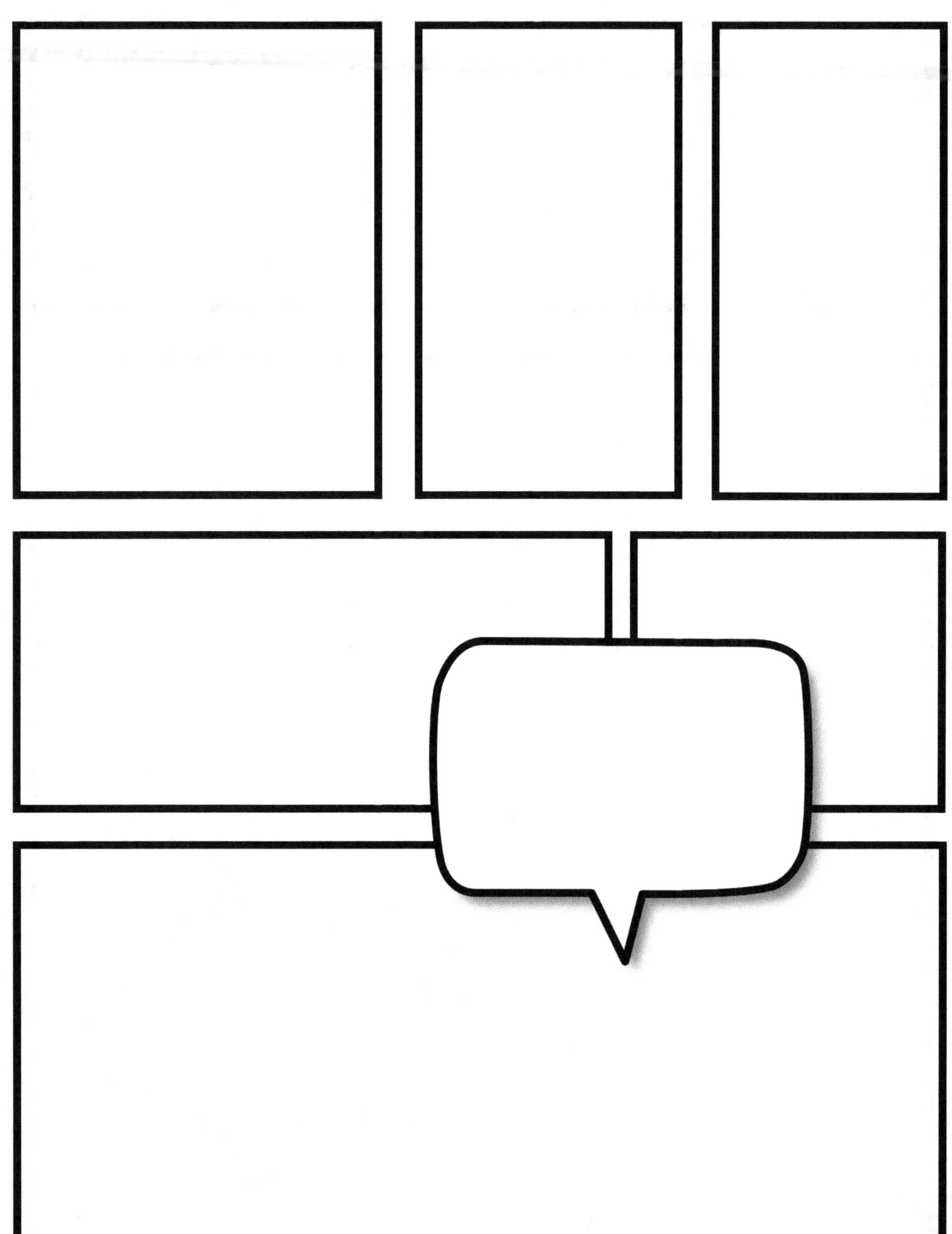

STORY TITLE:

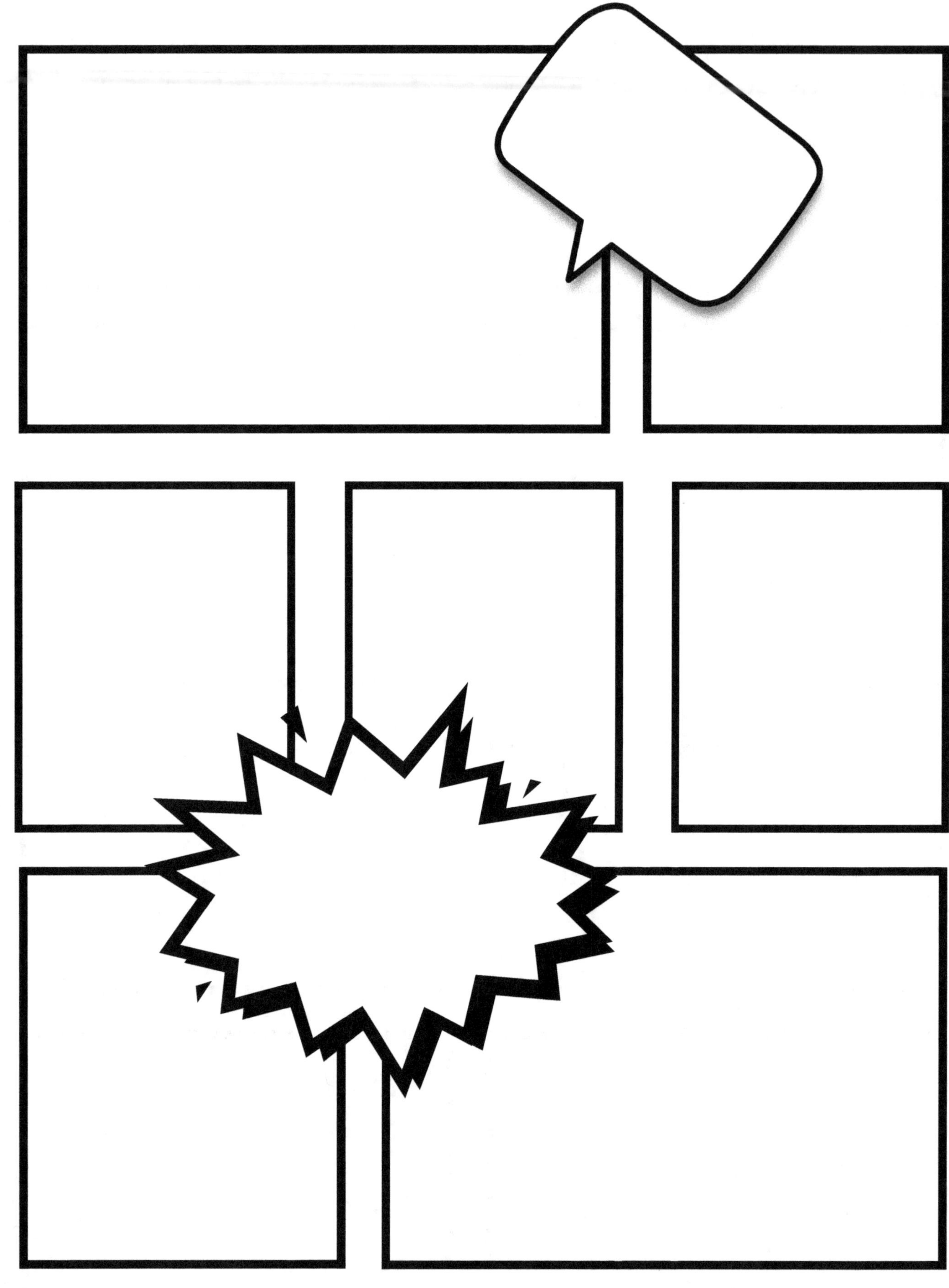

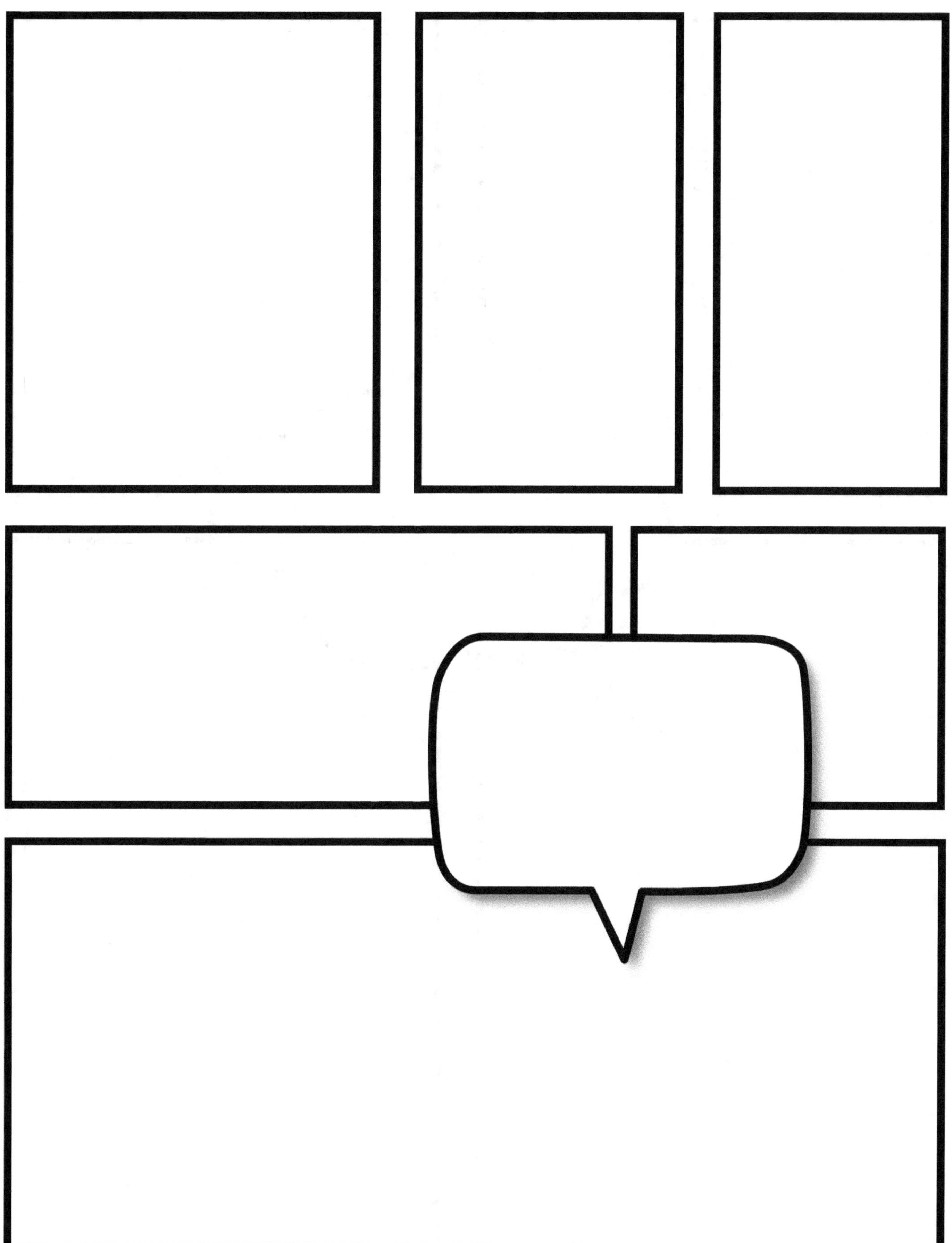

STORY TITLE:

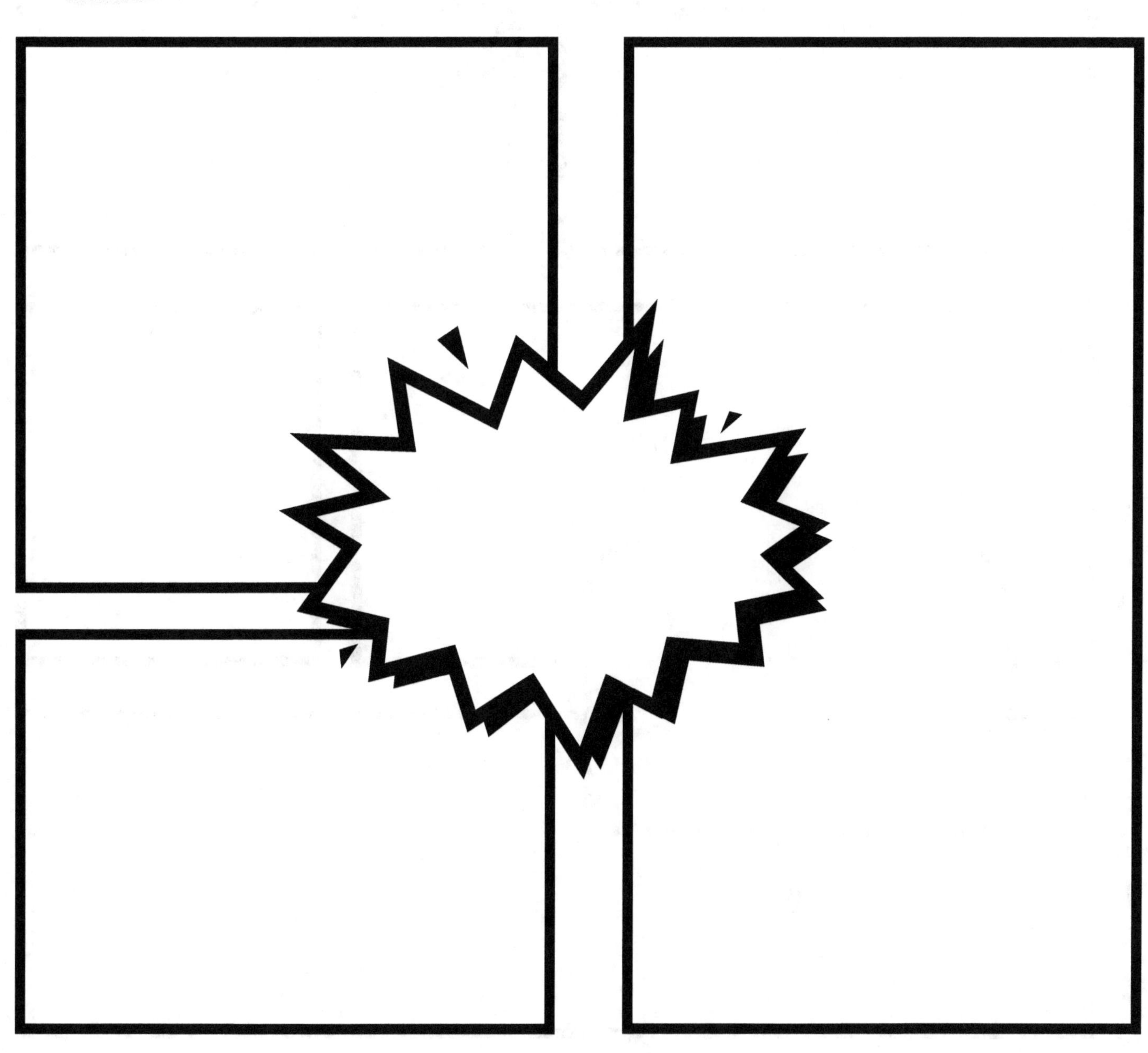

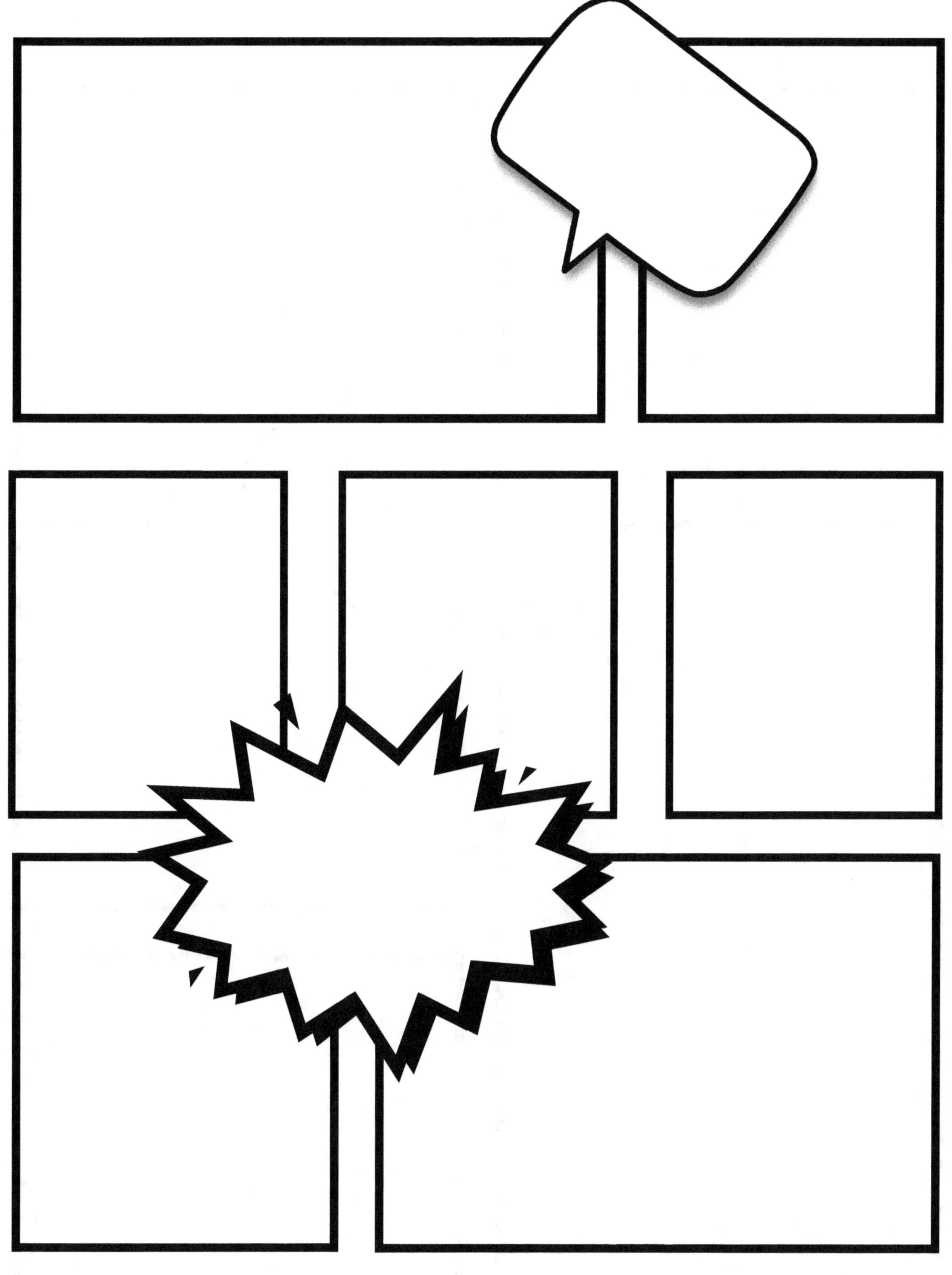

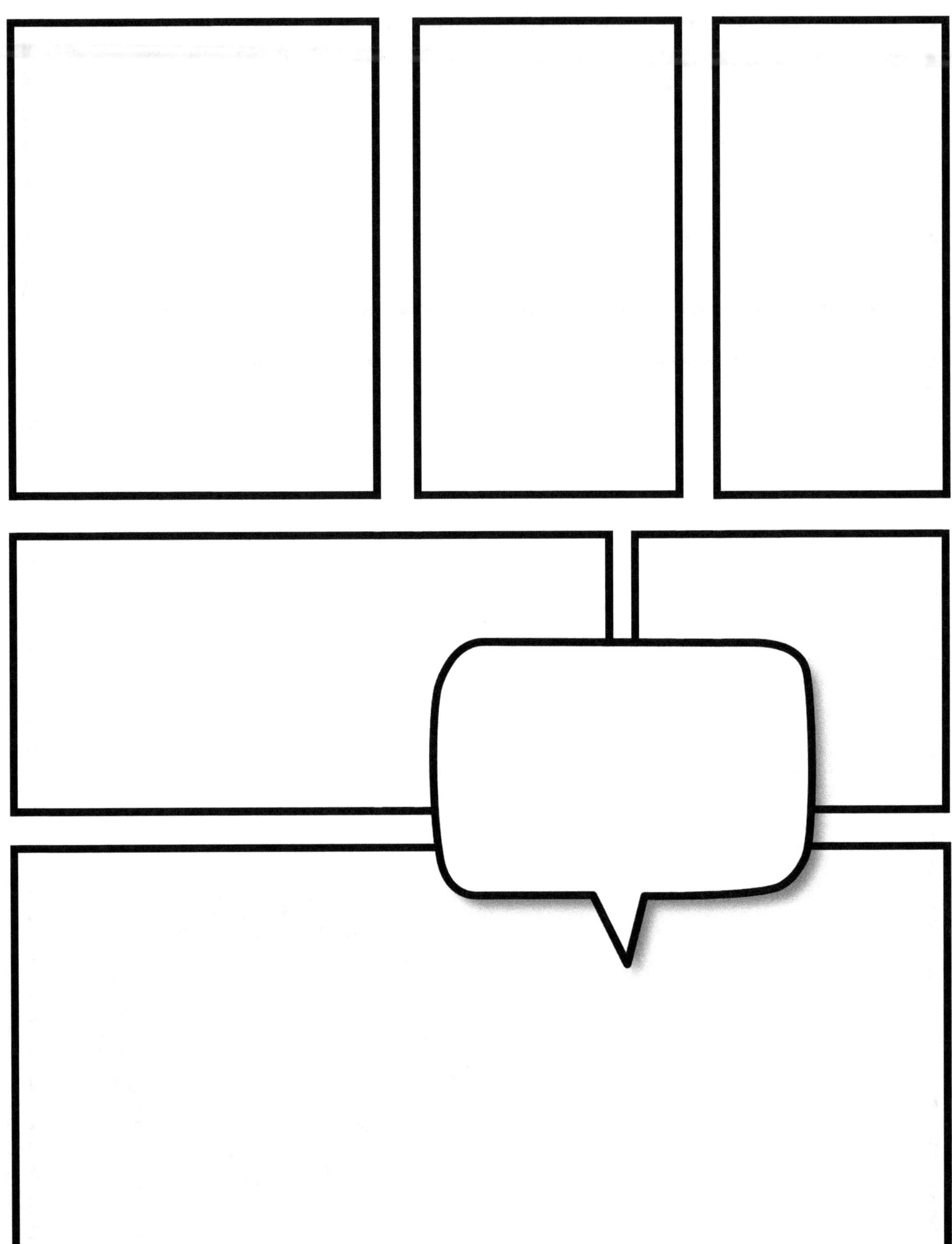

STORY TITLE:

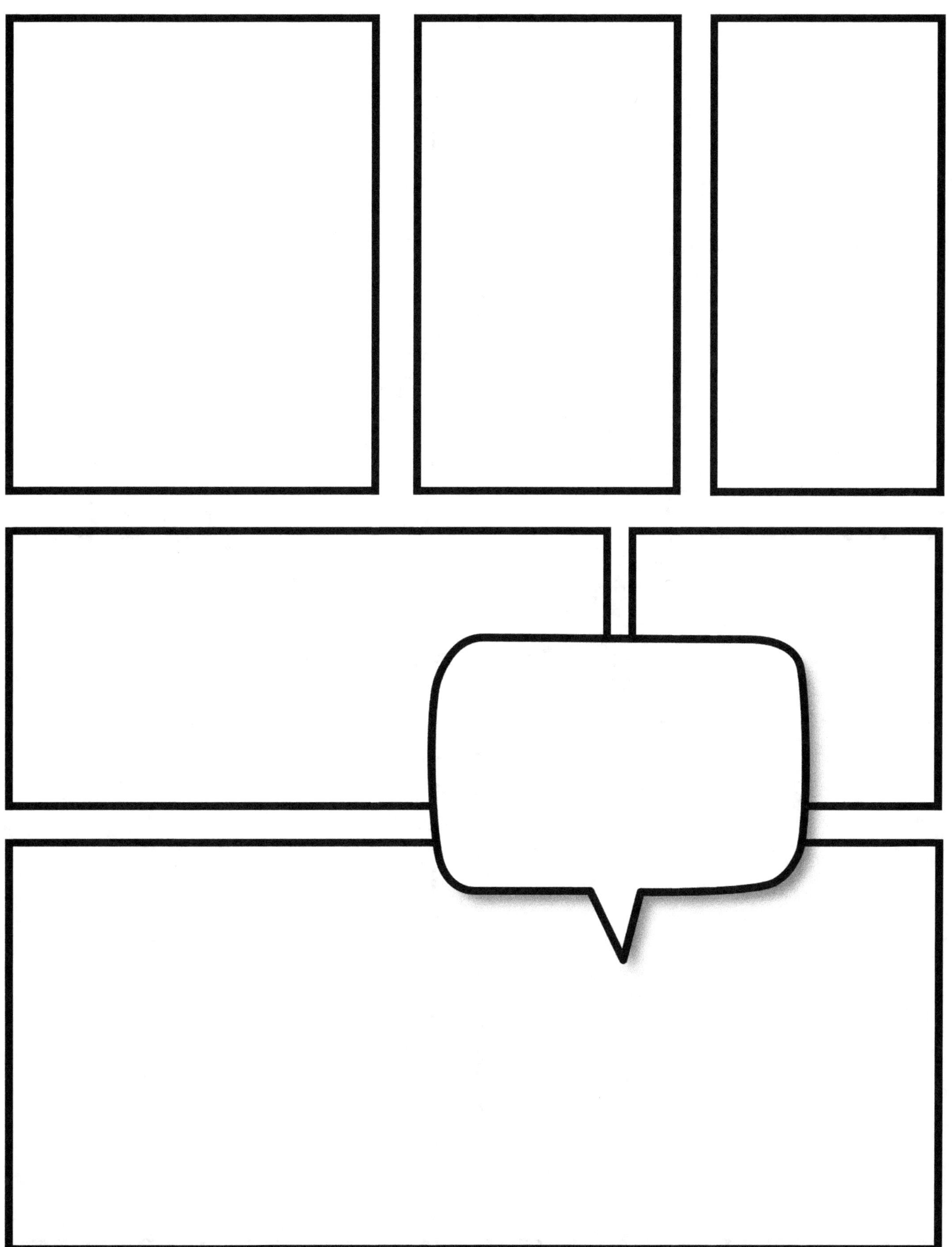

STORY TITLE:

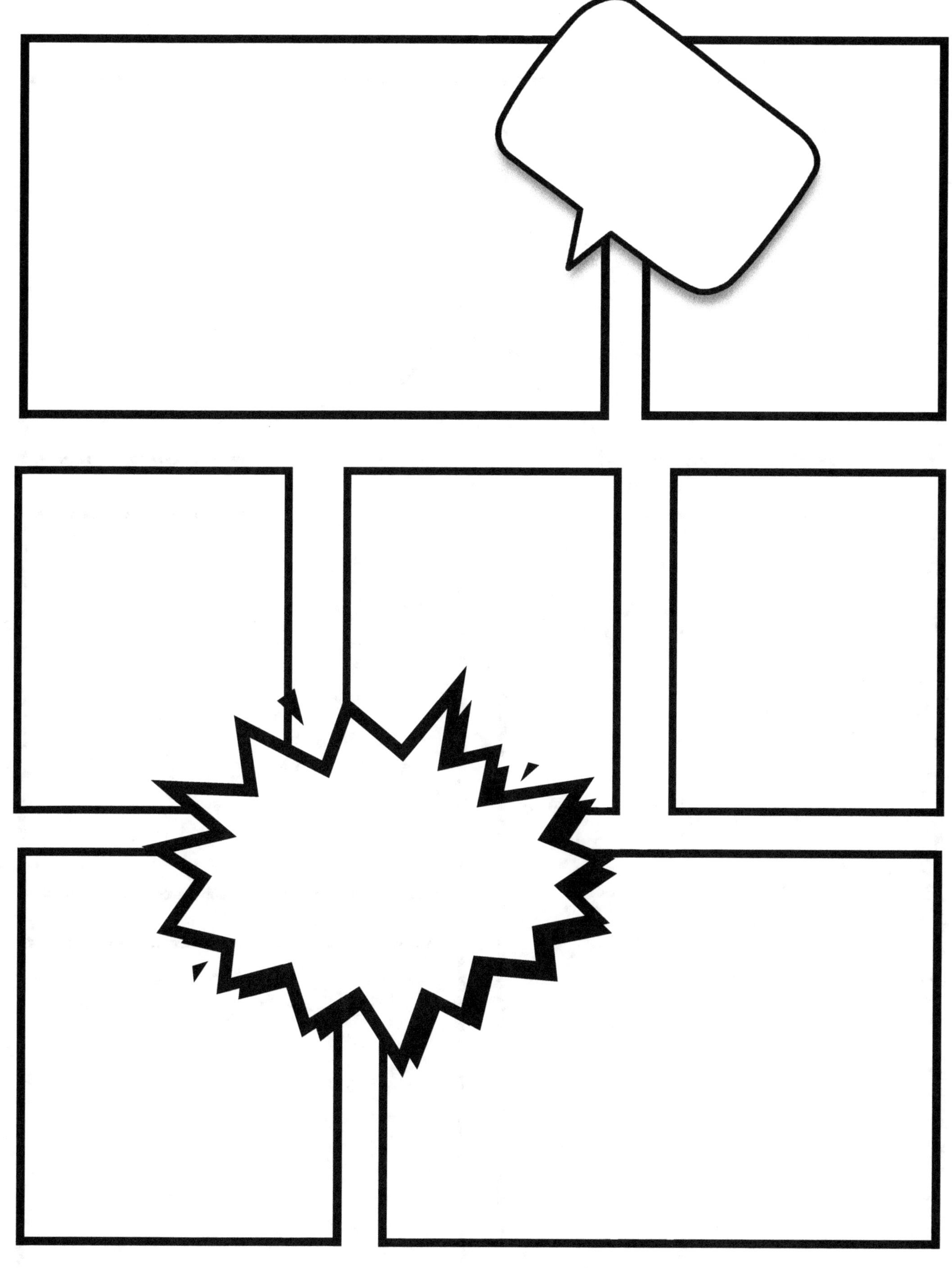

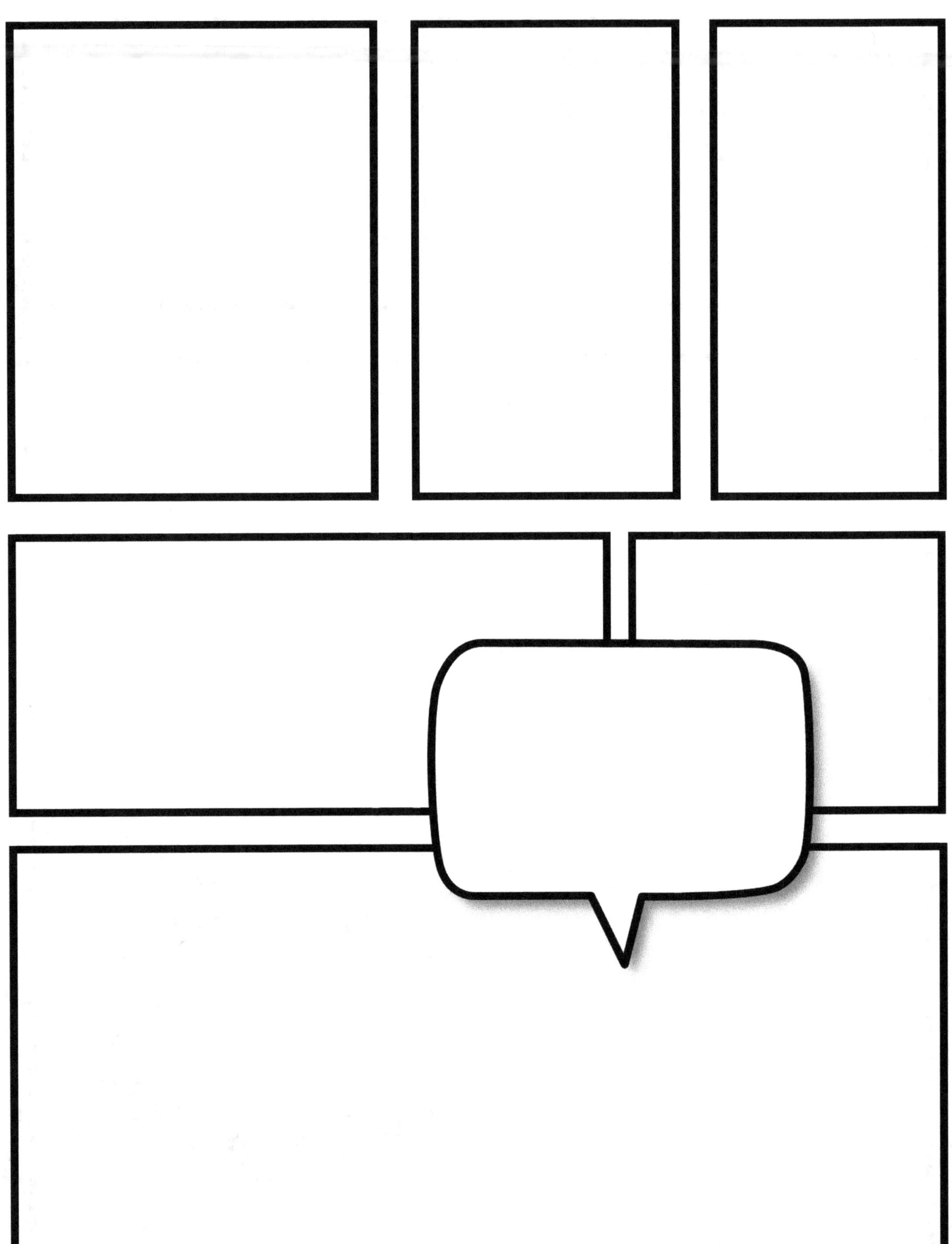

STORY TITLE:

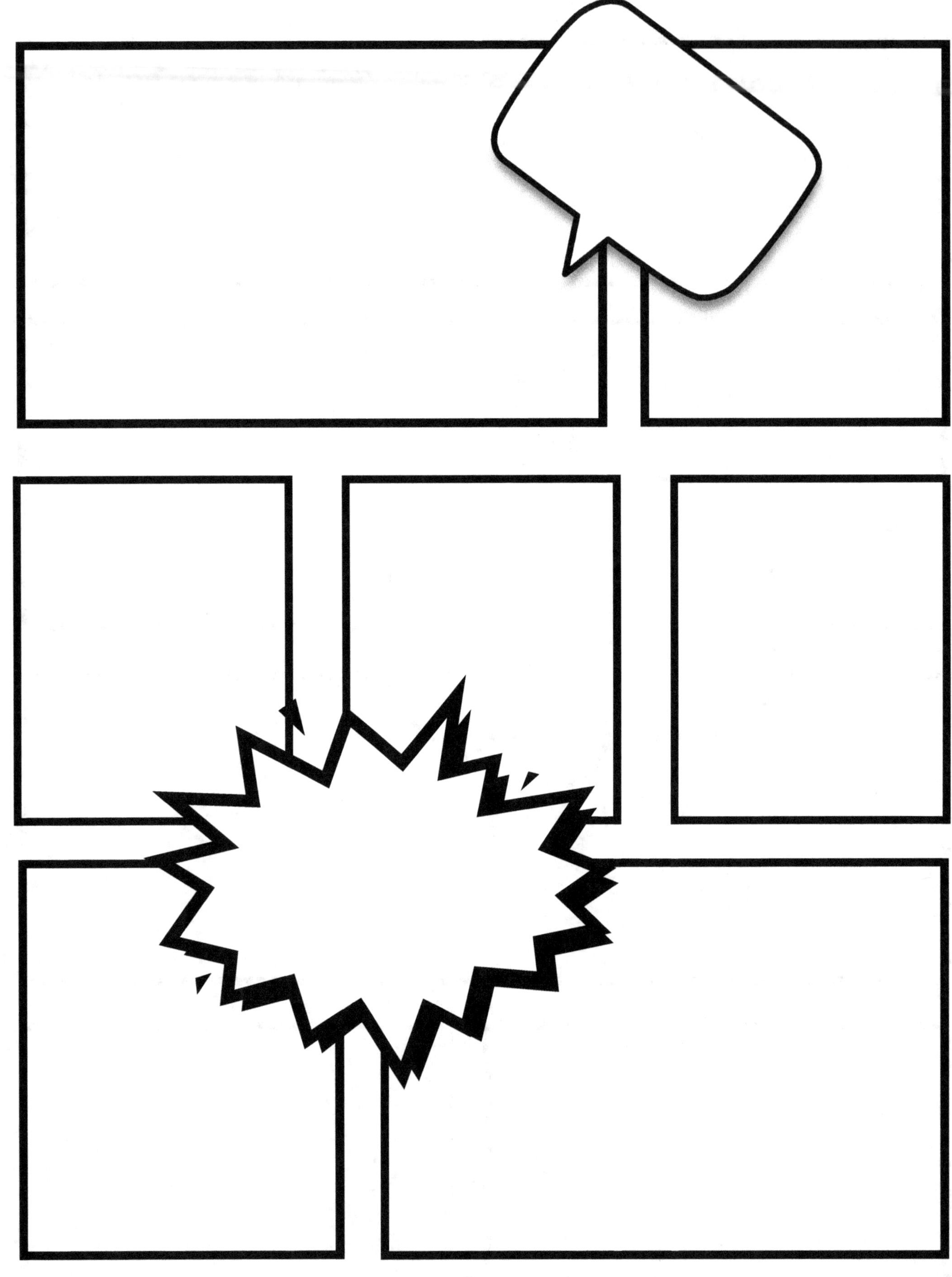

STORY TITLE:

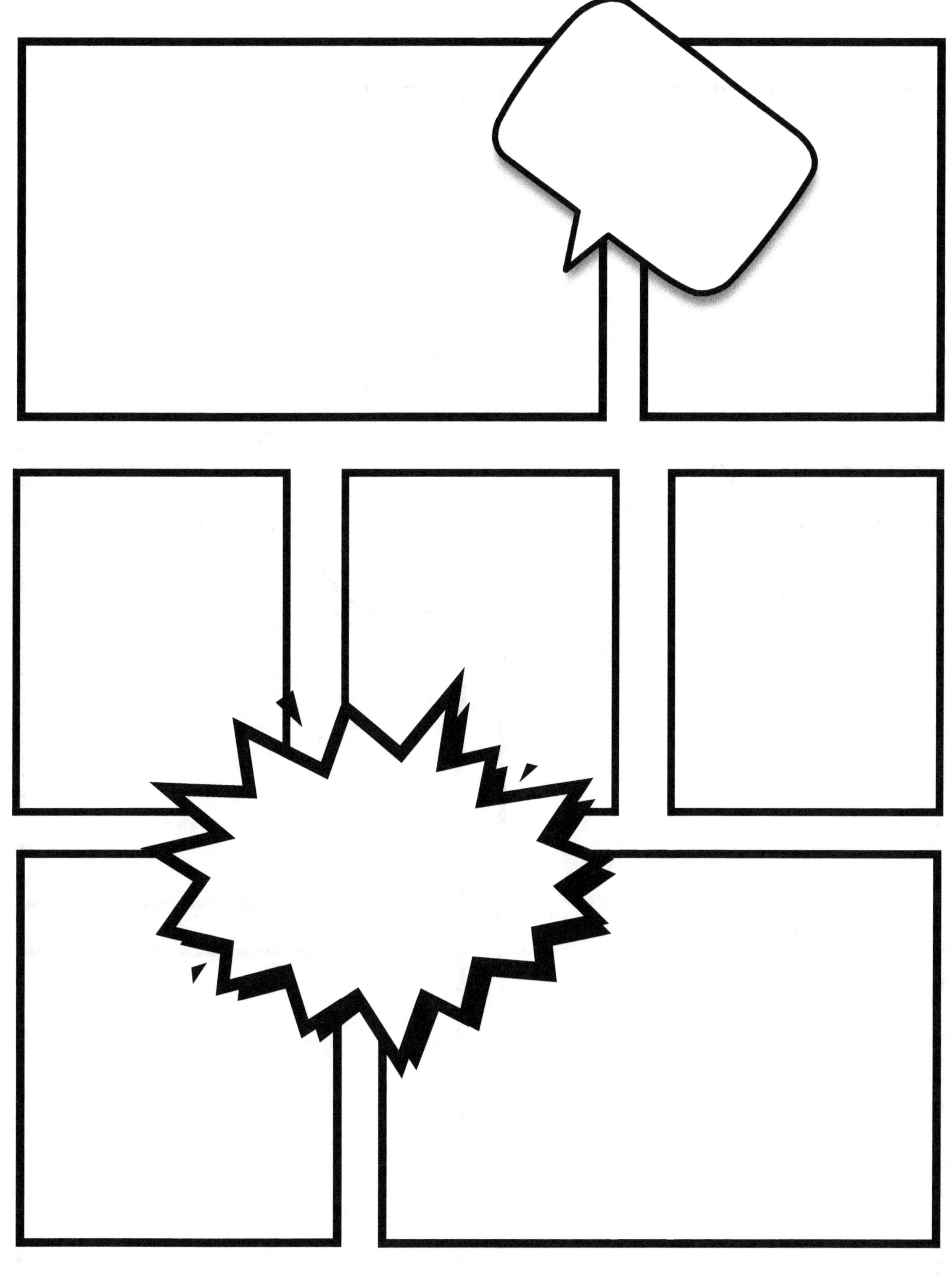

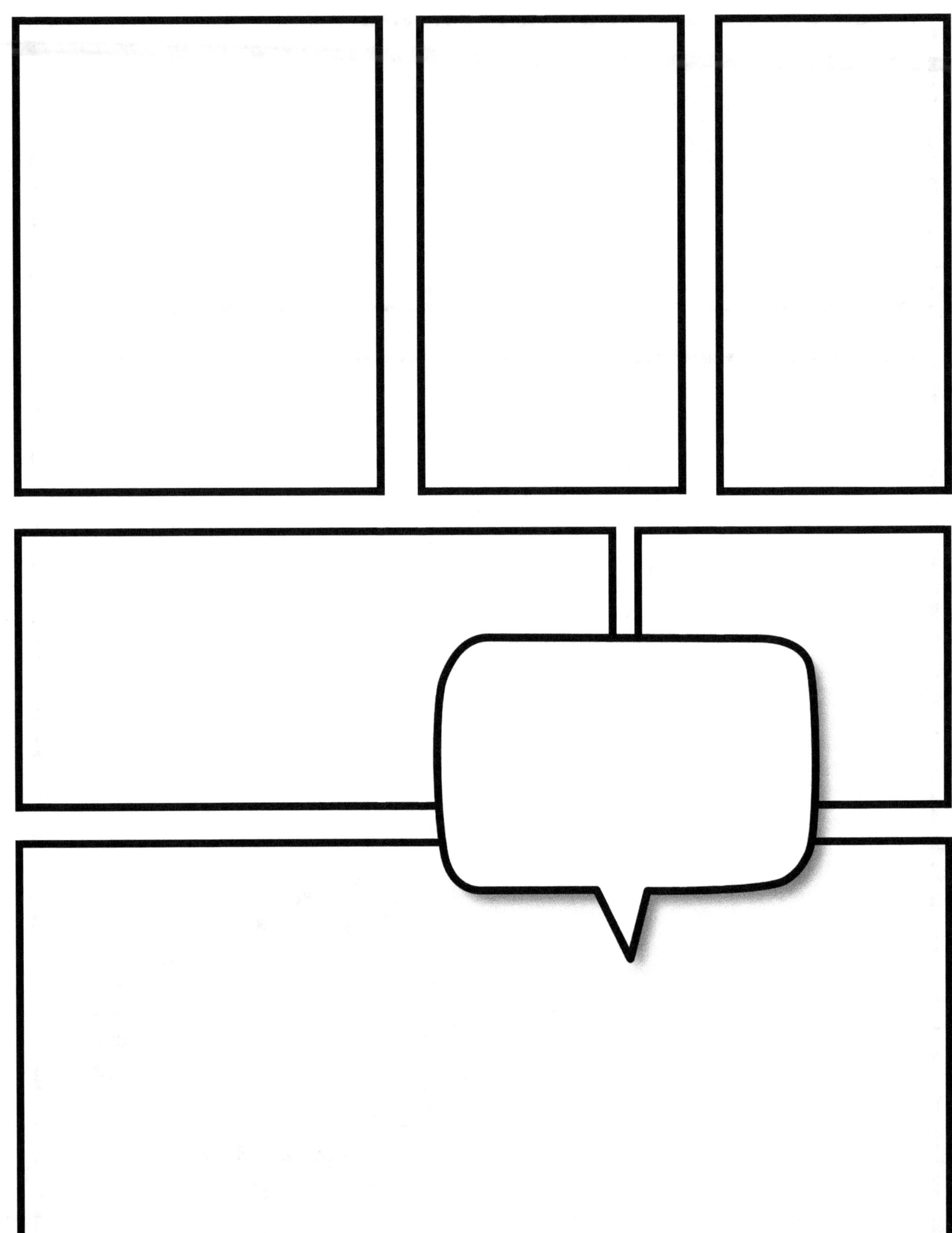

STORY TITLE:

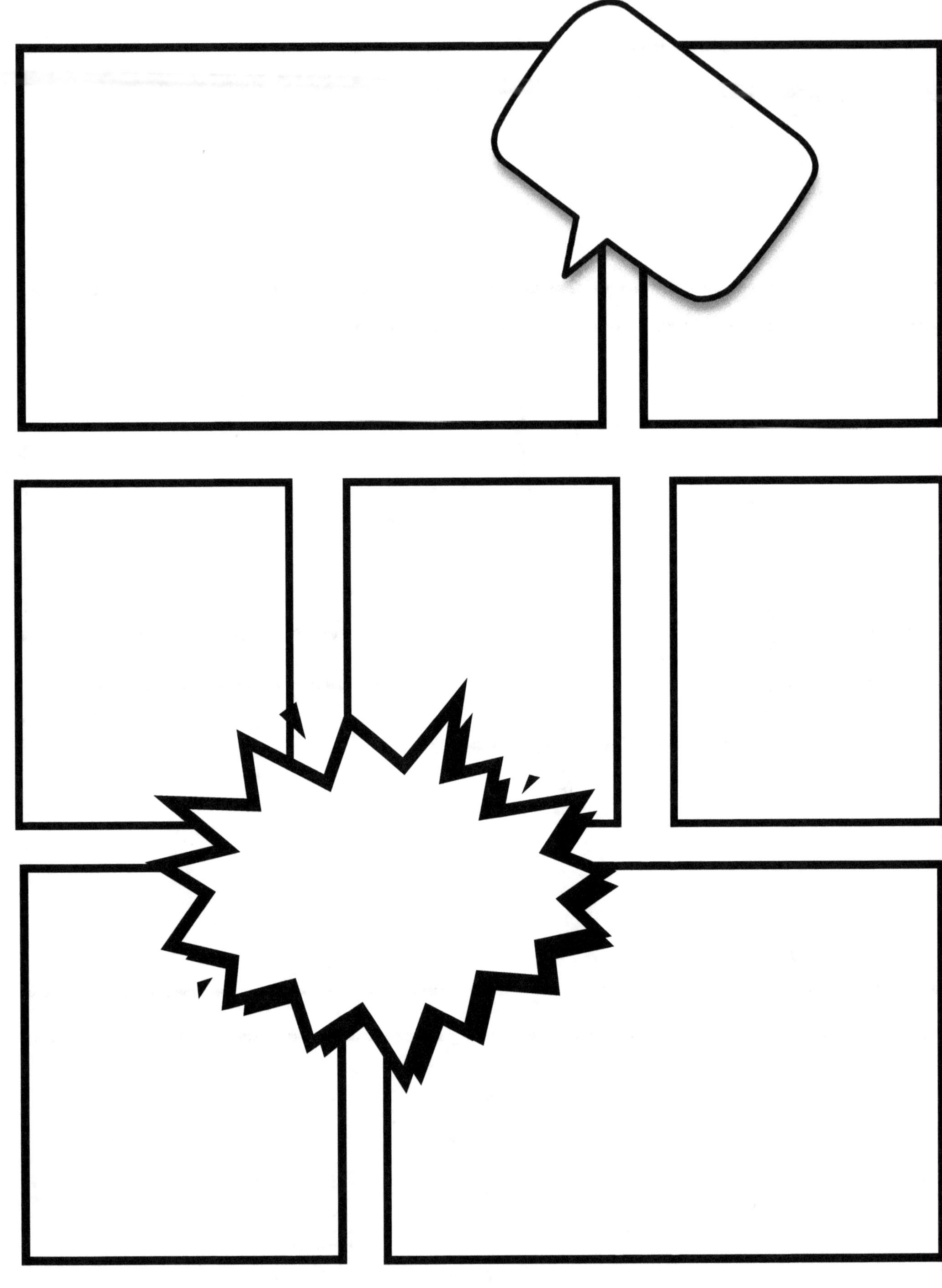